D0912993

One World Trade Center

Simon Rose

www.av2books.com

AV² provides enriched content that supplements and complements this book. Weigl's AV² books strive to create inspired learning and engage young minds in a total learning experience.

Your AV² Media Enhanced books come alive with...

Audio
Listen to sections of the book read aloud.

Key Words
Study vocabulary, and complete a matching word activity.

Video
Watch informative video clips.

Quizzes
Test your knowledge.

Embedded Weblinks
Gain additional information for research.

Slide Show
View images and captions, and prepare a presentation.

Try This!
Complete activities and hands-on experiments.

...and much, much more!

Go to **www.av2books.com**, and enter this book's unique code.

BOOK CODE

F11628

AV² by Weigl brings you media enhanced books that support active learning.

Published by AV² by Weigl
350 5th Avenue, 59th Floor
New York, NY 10118
Websites: www.av2books.com www.weigl.com

Library of Congress Control Number: 2013953160
ISBN 978-1-4896-0736-2 (hardcover)
ISBN 978-1-4896-0737-9 (softcover)
ISBN 978-1-4896-0738-6 (single user eBook)
ISBN 978-1-4896-0739-3 (multi-user eBook)

Printed in the United States of America in North Mankato, Minnesota
1 2 3 4 5 6 7 8 9 0 18 17 16 15 14

052014
WEP310514

Editor: Heather Kissock
Design: Terry Paulhus

Every reasonable effort has been made to trace ownership and to obtain permission to reprint copyright material. The publishers would be pleased to have any errors or omissions brought to their attention so that they may be corrected in subsequent printings.

Weigl acknowledges Getty Images, Corbis, Alamy, and Dreamstime as its primary image suppliers for this title.

Contents

What Is One World Trade Center?

The New York City skyline changed dramatically on September 11, 2001, when terrorists crashed two airliners into the Twin Towers of the World Trade Center. Within hours, the two skyscrapers crumbled to the ground. More than 2,000 people lost their lives that day. Many others were left with serious injuries. A state of shock descended on the city. However, as traumatic as the attack was, it was not long before New Yorkers began to plan ways to remember those who died and bring renewal to the area where the two buildings once stood.

One World Trade Center is the main building in New York's new World Trade Center complex. Originally called the Freedom Tower, One World Trade Center has been built as part of a plan to rebuild the area and provide a fitting memorial for the victims of the attack. The skyscraper is the tallest building in the complex. It soars above five other office towers as well as the September 11 Memorial and Museum, which pays tribute to the people who lost their lives on that tragic day.

Even though One World Trade Center was built to preserve the memory of the Twin Towers, it was not intended to replace them. The new tower has its own **footprint** and is located well away from the site of the two original buildings. Two large reflecting pools will be situated in the footprints of the Twin Towers. The area surrounding the pools will be a peaceful plaza decorated with trees.

One World Trade Center is the tallest building in New York City, the tallest in the Western Hemisphere, and the fourth tallest building in the world.

Snapshot of New York State

New York State is located in the northeastern part of the United States. It shares its southern border with New Jersey and Pennsylvania and its northern border with the Canadian provinces of Ontario and Quebec. Connecticut, Massachusetts, and Vermont lie to its east.

INTRODUCING NEW YORK

CAPITAL CITY: Albany

FLAG:

MOTTO: *Excelsior* (Ever Upward)

NICKNAME: The Empire State

POPULATION: 19,651,127 (2013 est.)

ADMITTED TO THE UNION: July 26, 1788

CLIMATE: Warm and humid summers with cold winters

SUMMER TEMPERATURE: Average of 82° Fahrenheit (28° Celsius)

WINTER TEMPERATURE: Average of –7° F (–22° C)

TIME ZONE: Eastern Standard Time (EST)

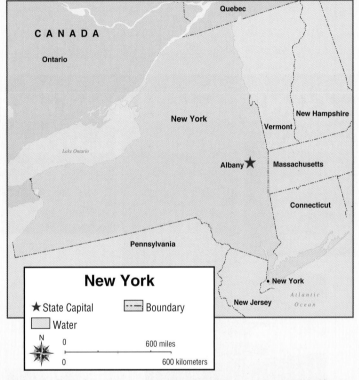

New York Symbols

New York has several official symbols. Some symbols represent the features that distinguish the area from other parts of the United States. Others indicate the unique place New York has in the history of the country.

OFFICIAL FLOWER
Rose

OFFICIAL BIRD
Eastern Bluebird

OFFICIAL TREE
Sugar Maple

A Step Back in Time

Following the terrorist attacks on September 11, there was no doubt that the city of New York would redevelop the World Trade Center site. However, much debate took place over what should be done with it. Some people wanted to preserve the area as a memorial to those who had died in the attacks. Others felt that the city should rebuild the Twin Towers. There was also a call to build a new World Trade Center with different buildings.

In November 2001, the Lower Manhattan Development Corporation (LMDC) was created. Its purpose was to decide the best way to redevelop the site.

CONSTRUCTION TIMELINE

December 19, 2003
The design for One World Trade Center is made public.

July 4, 2004
New York's mayor, Michael Bloomberg, lays the **cornerstone** for One World Trade Center.

April 27, 2006
Construction begins on One World Trade Center.

June 2006
After addressing security concerns in the original design, a revised design for One World Trade Center is unveiled.

December 19, 2006
The building's first steel columns are installed.

Michael Bloomberg was joined by New York Governor George Pataki and the governor of New Jersey, James McGreevey, at the laying of One World Trade Center's cornerstone.

The beams raised on December 19, 2006, were the first of 27 that would form the building's perimeter.

One of the first steps the LMDC took was to hold a design competition for the site. From the 2,000 entries received, the LMDC chose the design by **architect** Daniel Libeskind. Other architects were then selected to design specific buildings. The contract for One World Trade Center was awarded to David Childs.

The first beams were manufactured in Luxembourg from recycled steel. They ranged from 30 to 55 feet (9 to 16.7 meters) in length.

December 2009
One World Trade Center is now more than 200 feet (61 m) in height.

December 2010
Construction of the tower reaches the 52nd floor, which is the halfway point for the building's steel frame.

March 2012
The 100th floor of One World Trade Center is completed.

April 2012
One World Trade Center becomes the tallest building in New York, surpassing the Empire State Building.

May 10, 2013
The final section of the **spire** is added to the building's roof. One World Trade Center now reaches its final height of 1,776 feet (541 m).

The raising of the final piece of spire was considered a patriotic moment for the United States, symbolizing its victory over terrorism.

One World Trade Center's Location

The World Trade Center complex is located in the heart of Lower Manhattan's financial district. One World Trade Center itself sits in the northwest corner of the complex. It is close to both the World Financial Center and Wall Street.

When completed, the new World Trade Center complex will have six skyscrapers. The new complex also includes the Port Authority Trans-Hudson (PATH) Transportation Hub. The hub provides people commuting to and from offices in the World Trade Center with excellent access to transit, including the New York City subway system and Hudson River ferry terminals.

Construction of the new World Trade Center is scheduled for completion in 2016.

One World Trade Center Today

One World Trade Center is a symbol of hope and renewal for people throughout the United States. Although the building is still very new, it is already a major landmark on the New York City skyline. One World Trade Center is clearly visible from much of the surrounding area.

Height The tower is 1,776 feet (541 m) tall from the base to the top of the spire.

1,776 feet (541 m)

Floors The tower stands 104 stories above ground and 5 stories below ground.

Footprint The building's footprint is a 200 foot by 200 foot (61 m by 61 m) square. This is almost identical to the footprint of each of the Twin Towers at the original World Trade Center. The footprint covers an area of 40,000 square feet (3,716 sq. m).

Outside One World Trade Center

One World Trade Center is an easily recognizable part of the New York City skyline. There are a number of design elements that make the tower distinctive.

The Podium Base The tower rests on a 187-foot (57-m) high **podium**. The podium is made from **reinforced concrete** that has been covered with stainless steel panels and special blast-resistant glass. More than 4,000 glass pieces have been arranged to create a pattern on the podium. A reflective coating causes the pieces to glimmer when sunlight reaches them.

The podium rises 20 stories high from the ground.

One of the entrances faces the pedestrian mall where the 9/11 memorial is located.

Entrances People can access the building from all four sides through entrances that are 60 feet (18.3 m) high and up to 70 feet (21.3 m) wide. The west entrance takes visitors to the observation deck and transportation hub. The east entrance serves visitors to the restaurant at the top of the building, as well as office workers. The other entrances are also for people who work in the building.

Shape Eight isosceles triangles rise from the square podium. Four triangles point upwards, while the other four point down to the base. At the midpoint of the tower, the walls form an octagon. The top of the building becomes a square once again.

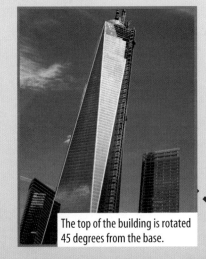
The top of the building is rotated 45 degrees from the base.

Spire The tower's spire is 408 feet (124.4 m) tall and weighs 758 tons (688 metric tons). At night, the spire is lit with hundreds of LED lights that form a beam of light visible from miles (kilometers) away. An aircraft-safety beacon also blinks from the spire.

The spire gave One World Trade the height needed to be named the tallest building in the United States.

The glass on the curtain wall is blast resistant. This protects the building and gives it additional strength.

Curtain Wall One World Trade Center appears to be a building made entirely of glass. The exterior walls are comprised of panels of insulated glass. Each panel measures 5 feet by 13 feet (1.5 m by 4 m) and spans the height of one building floor. These walls of glass allow sunlight to illuminate and warm the building during the day.

VIRTUAL TOUR

The height of One World Trade Center holds special meaning to Americans. The building is 1,776 feet (541 m) tall, and the United States declared its independence from Great Britain in 1776.

Inside One World Trade Center

One World Trade Center is one of New York City's leading business locations. The tower features office and retail space, a grand lobby, and a world-class observation deck offering spectacular views of New York City and the surrounding area.

Lobby The ground floor features a large, open lobby. The walls extend 55 feet (16.7 m) high, and natural light flows in from their windows. This creates a bright, airy public space. Art exhibits are displayed throughout the year, with the exhibits changing frequently to promote a vibrant environment.

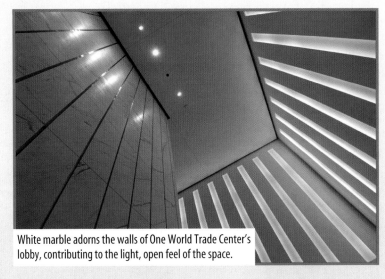

White marble adorns the walls of One World Trade Center's lobby, contributing to the light, open feel of the space.

The elevators at One World Trade Center travel at a speed of about 33 feet (10 m) per second.

Elevators One World Trade Center has 70 elevators. However, only 10 elevators travel directly from the lobby to the 104th floor. Five of these are service elevators that are used to carry large or heavy items. The other five are for people visiting the observation deck. People who work higher than the 64th floor take express elevators to one of the **sky lobbies**. From there, they board other elevators that reach the higher floors.

Observation Deck The One World Observatory covers approximately 120,000 square feet (11,148.4 sq m). At 1,250 feet (381 m) above street level, the observatory is located on floors 100 through 102. A glass **parapet** marks the heights of the Twin Towers at 1,362 feet (415 m) and 1,368 feet (417 m). Besides admiring the view, visitors can watch video presentations about the building, buy souvenirs at the gift shop, and have a bite to eat at the observatory's snack shops and restaurants.

On a clear day, the view from the observation deck can be up to 50 miles (80.5 km).

China Center has meeting rooms for a variety of functions, from small group meetings to trade fairs.

China Center Floors 64 to 69 are home to China Center, a conference center devoted to encouraging business between China and the United States. The China Center features meeting rooms, office suites, virtual offices, event spaces, and a restaurant. A private members club is found on the 66th floor. Here, club members have access to fine dining, spa services, and entertainment.

Office and Retail Space One World Trade Center has more than 3 million square feet (278,709 sq. m) of office floor space on 71 floors, as well as 55,000 square feet (5,110 sq. m) of underground retail space. Several companies and organizations have moved their operations into the building, including magazine publisher Condé Nast and the U.S. General Services Administration.

Prior to the building's opening, sample offices were set up to show potential tenants how the space could be used.

Big Ideas behind One World Trade Center

The designers of One World Trade Center wanted to build both a world-class office building and a fitting tribute to the previous buildings on the site. Due to the events that caused the construction of a new World Trade Center, safety and security were significant concerns for the designers. The designers also believed that building a **sustainable** structure was important.

For security reasons, the tower is situated 90 feet (27 m) away from West Street, a highway known for its heavy traffic.

Safety and Security

One World Trade Center's safety systems are highly advanced and exceed New York City Building Code standards. The building has a reinforced concrete base with no windows. This design feature will protect the base from a potential bomb attack or other large explosion. All elevator shafts, sprinkler systems, and stairwells are protected by reinforced concrete walls, which are 3 feet (91 centimeters) thick in most places. To allow large numbers of people to exit the building at one time, the emergency stairwells are extra-wide and **pressurized**. The building also has a stairwell that is reserved for firefighters in case of emergency.

Protecting the Environment

One World Trade Center is one of the world's most environmentally friendly buildings of its size. Much of the building is constructed from recycled materials, and more than 75 percent of its waste products are recycled. The building's windows contain ultra-clear glass to allow a large amount of sunlight into the office space. On very sunny days, the interior lights automatically dim, helping to reduce energy use.

Rainwater is collected and used in the tower's cooling systems.

Science at Work at One World Trade Center

The construction of One World Trade Center required planning, labor, and equipment. The people who built One World Trade Center used tools, materials, and methods that operated under basic scientific principles.

The building's vertical beams extend approximately 70 feet (21.3 m) into the ground.

Withstanding Weight

One World Trade Center's design team had to take **loads** into consideration when planning the building. The building's weight is supported by a group of vertical steel columns. Horizontal steel **girders** running between the vertical columns support each floor. The weight of the building is transferred from the girders to the vertical columns. Gravity pulls the weight downward to the area where the columns meet the building's base. The weight is then spread out across the building's **substructure**, distributing it over a wide area.

Reinforced Concrete

Concrete has many features that make it ideal for building skyscrapers. It is highly resistant to freezing and thawing, lasts a long time, and is watertight. All of this makes concrete very strong. To make it even stronger, builders often reinforce the concrete. One World Trade Center's base and core, for instance, are made of reinforced concrete.

When reinforcing concrete, metal bars are placed inside a mold, and concrete is added. Once the concrete sets, the bars bond to it. This strengthens the concrete and allows it to withstand the natural forces that act upon it, such as wind.

Concrete was also used for the building's floors and many of the interior walls.

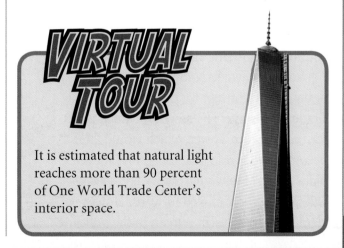

VIRTUAL TOUR

It is estimated that natural light reaches more than 90 percent of One World Trade Center's interior space.

One World Trade Center's Builders

Designing and building One World Trade Center required a team of construction professionals. The plan for the entire complex was the creation of one architect, while other architects designed the individual buildings. All of these architects relied on the skills of ironworkers, crane operators, concrete finishers, and people from many other trades to bring their visions to life.

One of Libeskind's more recent projects was the redesign of the Bundeswehr Military History Museum, in Dresden, Germany. The museum reopened in 2011 after years of reconstruction.

Daniel Libeskind Architect

Originally from Poland, Daniel Libeskind immigrated to the United States in 1964. He received his architecture degree in 1970 and then continued his studies in England, completing his post-graduate degree in 1972. Libeskind has been the architect for important projects in several different countries, including Germany, England, Canada, and Switzerland. In 2003, he designed the concept for the new World Trade Center site. His design included plans for the Freedom Tower, which would later become One World Trade Center. Libeskind's plans for the Freedom Tower were revised when the project moved forward. However, elements of his design remain in the building.

David Childs Architect

David Childs is a consulting design partner at Skidmore, Owings & Merrill's (SOM) New York office. In 2003, he was awarded the job of designing the building that was to become One World Trade Center. Childs is a graduate of Yale College and the Yale School of Art and Architecture. He joined the Washington, D.C. office of SOM in 1971 and served as chairman of the National Capital Planning Commission from 1975 to 1981. Childs moved to SOM's New York office in 1984. He has completed many major architectural projects in the United States and around the world.

David Childs also designed 7 World Trade Center. This was the first building in the new World Trade Center to open.

Ironworkers

Ironworkers are responsible for building, and sometimes dismantling, the steel frames of large buildings. They are the people who help to assemble the cranes that are used to lift steel girders into place. They also work closely with crane operators once construction begins. Ironworkers use both power tools and manual tools to bolt steel pieces together. Although they wear safety harnesses, ironworkers have one of the most dangerous jobs in the construction industry, especially when working on high-rise buildings.

Ironworkers often work at great heights. They must follow proper safety procedures to avoid injury on the construction site.

Crane Operators

Cranes play an important role in the building of any large structure. They are particularly important in the construction of skyscrapers. On construction sites, tower cranes are used to lift and move building materials, machinery, and heavy objects. Tower crane operators often work at great heights and need special training for their job. They communicate with workers on the ground or inside the building under construction with hand signals or by radio. Crane operators use equipment in their cab to move the crane around and to monitor the progress of the job.

Tower crane operators rely on the equipment inside the cab to move the crane, to communicate with people on the ground, and to monitor the job being done.

Concrete Finishers

Concrete finishers are construction workers who specialize in using concrete. They work on both indoor and outdoor projects. Concrete finishers pour wet concrete into casts, or molds, and spread it to a desired thickness, depending on the project. They then level and smooth the surfaces and edges of the concrete. Concrete finishers also repair, waterproof, and restore existing concrete surfaces. At One World Trade Center, concrete finishers worked on floors and walls throughout the tower.

Concrete finishers must have a solid understanding of pouring, leveling, setting, and finishing techniques.

Similar Structures around the World

Countries all over the world compete to build the world's tallest buildings and towers. One World Trade Center is one of the tallest office towers in the world, but there are taller buildings in other countries.

Burj Khalifa

BUILT: 2010
LOCATION: Dubai, United Arab Emirates
DESIGN: Adrian Smith, Skidmore, Owings & Merrill
DESCRIPTION: The Burj Khalifa is the world's tallest humanmade structure, at 2,717 feet (828 m). It was built to help Dubai attract new businesses and to promote Dubai as a world-class city. The building has both office and residential space. The highest occupied floor is at 1,916 feet (584 m). An observation deck makes up the building's 124th floor.

The Burj Khalifa has more than 160 stories. This is more than any other building in the world.

The Makkah Clock Royal Tower is the world's tallest clock tower and has the largest clock face in the world.

Makkah Clock Royal Tower

BUILT: 2012
LOCATION: Mecca, Saudi Arabia
DESIGN: Dar Al-Handasah
DESCRIPTION: The Makkah Clock Royal Tower is a hotel in the Abraj Al Bait Towers. At 1,972 feet (601 m), the tower is the tallest building in Saudi Arabia and the third-tallest **freestanding** structure in the world. It is located beside the Al-Masijd Al-Haram mosque, which is Islam's most sacred site. The hotel provides accommodation for the many pilgrims that travel to Mecca each year as part of the Hajj.

Taipei 101

BUILT: 2004
LOCATION: Taipei, Taiwan
DESIGN: C.Y. Lee and Partners
DESCRIPTION: Taipei 101 is 1,667 feet (508 m) high and was the tallest building in the world from 2004 to 2010. The tower's designers were inspired by historic Chinese buildings and built Taipei 101 to resemble a Chinese pagoda. The building has an indoor observation area on the 89th floor and an outdoor observation deck on the 91st floor. Its double-deck elevators are currently the fastest in the world.

Construction costs for Taipei 101 were more than $1.7 billion USD.

Petronas Towers

BUILT: 1994
LOCATION: Kuala Lumpur, Malaysia
DESIGN: César Pelli
DESCRIPTION: The Petronas Towers were the world's tallest buildings from 1998 to 2004. At 1,483 feet (452 m), they are still the world's tallest twin buildings. The buildings' design comes from different aspects of Malaysian culture. However, the towers also had to be designed to cope with Malaysia's volatile weather. Each tower was built to withstand winds up to 84 miles (135 km) per hour. A double decker skybridge connects the two towers on the 41st and 42nd floors. The bridge's design allows the towers to move independently when they sway in high winds. This prevents the bridge from breaking.

The Petronas Towers are home to shopping and entertainment venues, as well as a mosque, symphony hall, museum, and conference center.

Issues Facing One World Trade Center

Building One World Trade Center required a great deal of planning. Some planning concerns were typical to architects who design high skyscrapers. Other concerns were related specifically to One World Trade Center.

WHAT IS THE ISSUE?

Due to its height, One World Trade Center is subject to extremely strong winds.	As a public building, anyone can access One World Trade Center.

EFFECTS

The high winds could cause the tower to sway too far and be so badly damaged that it could collapse.	The security of people inside the building could be at risk.

ACTION TAKEN

One World Trade Center has been designed to withstand powerful winds. The tower's **chamfered** edges decrease the effects of high winds, resulting in less building sway.	One World Trade Center has been set up with extensive security features, including more than 400 closed-circuit security cameras and computer-controlled security doors. Elevators have passenger identification controls. People will only have access to the floors on which they work.

Build a Skyscraper

Building a skyscraper takes much planning. One of the key considerations when planning a very tall building is its stability. Architects and designers must use materials that will support the weight of the building at all levels. These materials must be positioned so that they will hold that weight over the long term.

Try the following activity to learn about the planning architects do when designing a building. See if you can design a skyscraper out of newspaper that will withstand the force of a light breeze.

Materials
• Several sheets of newspaper
• Tape
• Safety scissors
  (optional)
• Notebook
• Pen or pencil

Instructions
1. Begin manipulating the newspaper to see if you can make it stronger. You can try twisting it, folding it, rolling it, cutting it, and packing it. Which process do you think will help you make a sturdy structure?

2. Once you have decided how you want to use the paper, draw a plan for your skyscraper in your notebook. Your plan should show how you are going to position the paper to achieve maximum strength and height.

3. Prepare your sheets of newspaper according to your plan, and begin placing them in position. Tape the pieces together when needed.

4. Once you have completed building your skyscraper according to your drawing, stand back and fan it with your notebook. Does it remain stable, or does it begin to fall apart? What could be done to make it stronger?

5. Continue to experiment with your skyscraper. How high can you make a building of newspaper before it becomes unstable?

One World Trade Center Quiz

Q How tall is One World Trade Center?

A 1,776 feet (541 m)

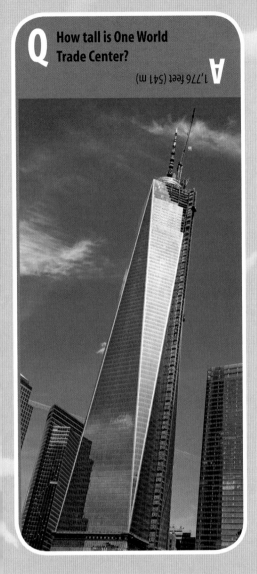

Q Who was the architect of One World Trade Center?

A David Childs

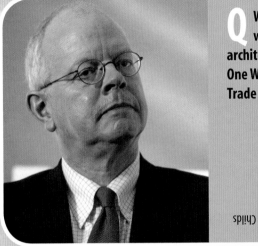

Q What three key shapes are found in One World Trade Center's design?

A Triangles, squares, and octagons

Q How fast do the Observation Deck elevators travel?

A 33 feet (10 m) per second

Key Words

architect: a professional who designs and supervises the construction of buildings or other large structures

chamfered: having a sloping edge

cornerstone: a stone laid at a ceremony commemorating the origin of a building

footprint: the surface space occupied by a structure or device

freestanding: not supported by another structure

girders: large iron or steel beams

loads: weights or sources of pressure carried by an object

parapet: a low wall at the end of a platform or roof

podium: a low wall or platform forming a base for a structure

pressurized: designed to maintain normal air pressure

reinforced concrete: concrete that has metal bars embedded in it to add strength

sky lobbies: floors in a building that serve as an interchange between lower and higher elevators

spire: a tapering structure at the top of a building

substructure: the underlying or supporting part of a structure

sustainable: capable of being maintained with minimal effect on the environment

Index

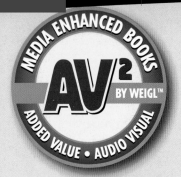

Log on to www.av2books.com

AV² by Weigl brings you media enhanced books that support active learning. Go to www.av2books.com, and enter the special code found on page 2 of this book. You will gain access to enriched and enhanced content that supplements and complements this book. Content includes video, audio, weblinks, quizzes, a slide show, and activities.

AV² Online Navigation

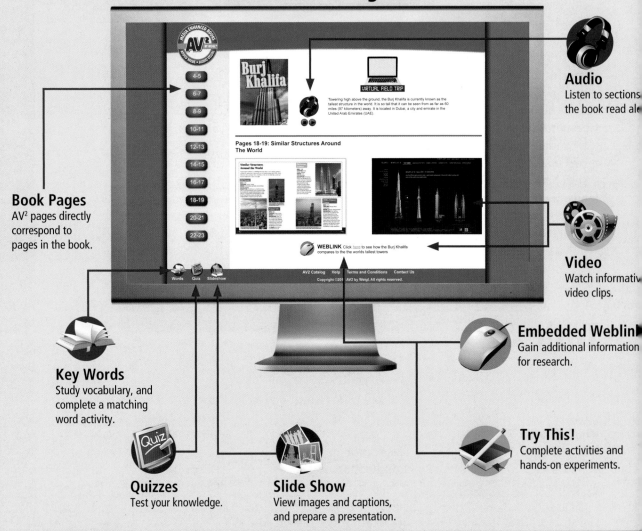

Audio
Listen to sections the book read al

Book Pages
AV² pages directly correspond to pages in the book.

Video
Watch informativ video clips.

Embedded Weblin
Gain additional information for research.

Key Words
Study vocabulary, and complete a matching word activity.

Try This!
Complete activities and hands-on experiments.

Quizzes
Test your knowledge.

Slide Show
View images and captions, and prepare a presentation.

AV² was built to bridge the gap between print and digital. We encourage you to tell us what you like and what you want to see in the future.

Sign up to be an AV² Ambassador at www.av2books.com/ambassador.